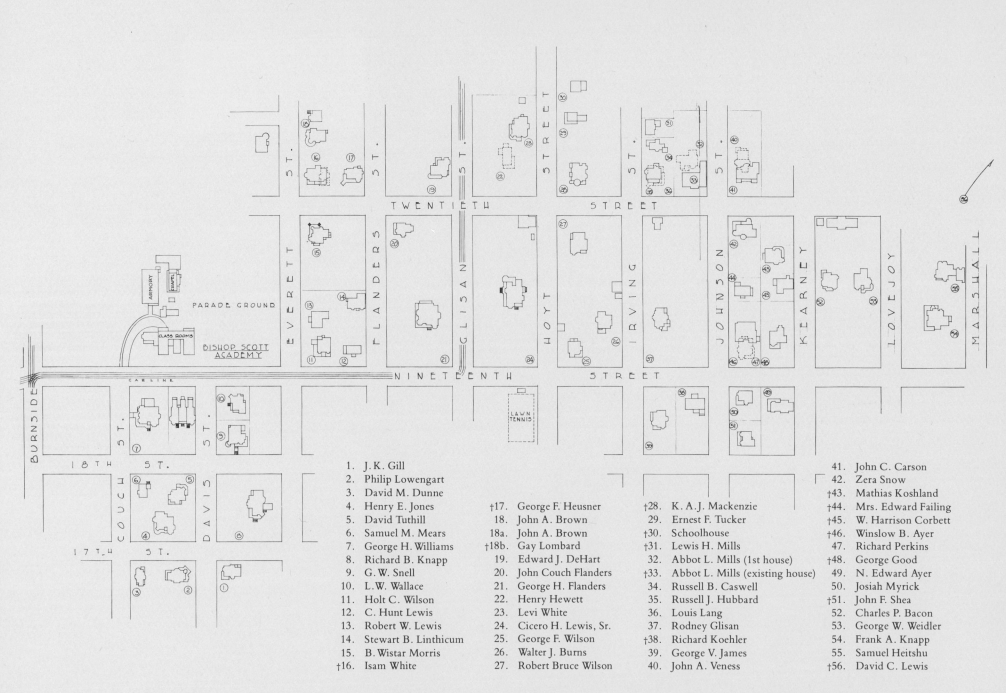

1. J. K. Gill
2. Philip Lowengart
3. David M. Dunne
4. Henry E. Jones
5. David Tuthill
6. Samuel M. Mears
7. George H. Williams
8. Richard B. Knapp
9. G. W. Snell
10. L. W. Wallace
11. Holt C. Wilson
12. C. Hunt Lewis
13. Robert W. Lewis
14. Stewart B. Linthicum
15. B. Wistar Morris
†16. Isam White

†17. George F. Heusner
18. John A. Brown
18a. John A. Brown
†18b. Gay Lombard
19. Edward J. DeHart
20. John Couch Flanders
21. George H. Flanders
22. Henry Hewett
23. Levi White
24. Cicero H. Lewis, Sr.
25. George F. Wilson
26. Walter J. Burns
27. Robert Bruce Wilson

†28. K. A. J. Mackenzie
29. Ernest F. Tucker
†30. Schoolhouse
†31. Lewis H. Mills
32. Abbot L. Mills (1st house)
†33. Abbot L. Mills (existing house)
34. Russell B. Caswell
35. Russell J. Hubbard
36. Louis Lang
37. Rodney Glisan
†38. Richard Koehler
39. George V. James
40. John A. Veness

41. John C. Carson
42. Zera Snow
†43. Mathias Koshland
†44. Mrs. Edward Failing
†45. W. Harrison Corbett
†46. Winslow B. Ayer
47. Richard Perkins
†48. George Good
49. N. Edward Ayer
50. Josiah Myrick
†51. John F. Shea
52. Charles P. Bacon
53. George W. Weidler
54. Frank A. Knapp
55. Samuel Heitshu
†56. David C. Lewis

†still standing

NINETEENTH STREET

NINETEENTH STREET

Richard Marlitt

OHS: 1978

LC 78-73291
ISBN 0-87595-000-0

Revised Edition
1978
© Oregon Historical Society

(First Edition published, 1968)

AMERICAN CITIES since the turn of the century have grown at such a furious pace that all forms of past existence are being completely erased. Great sections of metropolitan areas have been torn down, rebuilt, replaced, rejuvenated or ruined. Few of the residences shown in this book are standing today. Even the street scenes are barely recognizable. The photographic collection presented here shows the environment of a people who became successful in a new land, in surroundings that express a leisure and refinement that came with success. Only the backdrops of these pictures show a raw western scene. The landscaping, the interior views, and the houses themselves had an elegance and taste that matched any similar long-established city of the eastern seaboard.

The area has completely changed in character. Nineteenth Street today is a busy one-way thoroughfare that carries heavy traffic through the northwest district toward Portland's city center, Canyon Road and the freeways. There is little left to show that once it was the city's most elegant avenue. Stretching from Burnside Street to approximately Marshall Street and encompassing a block or two on either side was every form of nineteenth century architecture. At first there were simple box-like structures only once removed from a New England farmhouse. Later were built the Italianate villas whose Florentine rustication was reproduced in wood. Then came the great piles of the Gothic Victorian era, heavy with jigsaw, stained glass, and stick-style ornament. Some of them were faintly related to the French chateaux, others to the turreted Germanic castles. After the Mansard fronts came the heavy stone and shingle Richardsonian style, and then the handsome Georgian mansions.

This was the city's fashionable section in which to live and Nineteenth Street was its thoroughfare. Tree-lined and remote from the commercial river front, it had an aura of respectability and permanence. From 1849 it had been the donation land claim of Captain John Couch, who at that time laid out a block system along the river front. In the 1870s he extended the streets into this area and opened it to development. It was intended to be residential in character and remained so until the First World War, some of the houses dating as late as 1912. From that time on it was impossible to hold back the spreading business district or the change of living patterns of the post-war years, especially the immediate access made possible by the automobile to areas away from the central district. One by one the great houses succumbed and today there are but a handful left, mostly remodelled for professional or commercial use.

The story of Nineteenth Street is typical of the American scene. Only a geographic quirk could have kept such an area in a residential character.

RICHARD MARLITT
PORTLAND, 1978

This Panorama, published in the West Shore *magazine in 1888, starts us in the southeastern end of the area. From the grounds of the Snell residence at Eighteenth and Davis streets we look easterly across the rear of the Knapp mansion and its block-square grounds. To the right of it is the J. K. Gill house facing Davis Street. Across from it, with the prominent tower is the residence of the Philip Lowengarts. In the right foreground is the David Tuthill residence almost hiding Dr. Henry E. Jones' home behind it. (This block is now occupied by St. Mary's Cathedral.) Beyond are the towers of Portland High School and the business district. The last house to the extreme right is the Samuel M. Mears residence. In the background are the square-riggers in the harbor, the foothills of the Cascades and Mt. Hood.*

This is an interesting picture with the handsome carriages, the well-dressed ladies, the careful landscaping, and the comfortable houses. Not a thing shown here existed thirty years before, except the fencing of a donation land claim.

CHASE LOWENGART JONES TUTHILL MEARS

THIS IS A VIEW of Seventeenth Street looking north from Couch Street that makes a good companion to the Panorama. In the distance is the front of the J. K. Gill house, in the center the side and rear of the Lowengart house, and to the right the residence of David M. Dunne.

The Gill and Lowengart houses have been gone for many years and the Dunne house, always occupied by the same family, finally made way in 1960 for the new Cathedral School. Seventy-five years ago the nearby neighbors, Dr. Henry E. Jones and his stepdaughter and her husband, Mr. and Mrs. Washburn, posed for this picture in front of the Dunne residence. There was very little to the west of this when the house was built. The dirt streets and wood sidewalks testify that it was the edge of town. But this picture, better than many others, shows that these houses of the eighties had an atmosphere of pleasant comfort and a leisurely way of living that disappeared in later years.

A photograph of the Dunne residence taken about 1892.

THIS IS A VERY OLD PHOTOGRAPH of the J.K. Gill house, the center house in the Panorama. It was unusual to have a whole house of this period done in shingles. The little patches of stucco with a parging pattern in them were the only relief. Another unusual feature was the divided window panes, rather like a colonial house.

J.K. Gill was a Yorkshireman who came to Oregon in 1866. The bookstore he established still bears his name. The little girl standing in the front yard is Mr. Gill's daughter, Dorothy Gill Montgomery.

In 1896 the Gills moved and the place became the home of the Henry Wessinger family. They lived in it until 1928 when they developed a family group of residences in Dunthorpe.

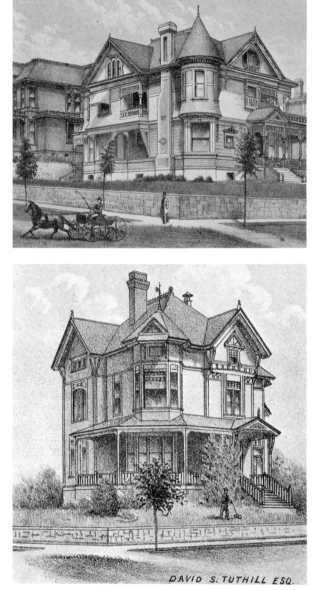

DAVID S. TUTHILL ESQ.

THIS GASLIT MANSION was built by George W. Snell, a successful druggist of the eighties. The front lawn facing Eighteenth Street is the spot from which the Panorama was taken. In 1898 it became the home of the Henry Wagners. In the war years its fine rooms housed transient boarders and in 1954 the typical story ended in an auction of stained glass windows, paneling and fireplaces, before demolition.

ON THE OPPOSITE CORNER from the Snell house was the residence of David Tuthill, the vice president of the Columbia River Paper Co. The wet, cold, winter scene on the opposite page shows how large and overbearing these houses could be. In 1903 it became the home of Walter Thomas Williamson, who had been the physician for the State Hospital in Salem. He was one of the area's leading neurologists and his career was topped by becoming the first West Coast trustee of the American Medical Association. This house and the others on the block came down when St. Mary's Cathedral was built on the site.

14

THE RICHARD B. KNAPP RESIDENCE erected on the block of Seventeenth, Eighteenth, Davis and Everett streets, was probably the most elaborate home in Portland. Exotic woods, rare stained glass, and hand-wrought hardware were used throughout. The cost of eighty thousand dollars in 1882 placed the structure in a category all its own. The Knapps' only son Lawrence became the son-in-law of Judge Bellinger. Benefactors of the Catholic Church, it would please the Knapps to know that the site is now the playground of St. Mary's School.

Richard Knapp was the partner of Knapp, Burrell & Co., an implement and machinery company. He and Mrs. Knapp filled the house with fine things from both Europe and the Orient. All the door hardware was fashioned in hand-hammered brass, the doors themselves being inlaid teak-wood. Each stained glass window had its own floral design. There were satin draperies edged with Belgian lace and the drawing room had an Aubusson rug woven in France to the dimensions of the room. The third floor was a ballroom with a stage for entertainments. Behind this was a billiard room.

Mr. and Mrs. Knapp separated and later the fortune dwindled. The bank that received the property leased it to the Parker F. Morey family who lived in the house for ten years until it was purchased by a Mr. and Mrs. Wilson. St. Mary's Cathedral purchased the property from the Wilsons' heirs and the house was dismantled in the late forties.

A very early view of the Knapp house when it was first occupied. The Williams house is to the far left. Notice the elephants at the front steps. The tower is particularly well defined in this view.

The interiors of the Knapp residence were works of art, from the coffered ceiling of the third floor ballroom to the elaborate wash—stands and hand-painted bathtubs.

All the fireplace tiles were designed and fired for each fireplace. The fireplace to the left was a strange design with a window over the mantel. Oddly enough this happened more than once in the house.

Victorian ornamental design has a distinctive character very much its own. The quarter shell, the tiny railings, the Gothic cupboard heads, matching buttresses dividing the counter, all are characteristics of the style.

The casing around the opening of the lower picture is a typical Victorian one and only a Victorian interior would reproduce the amazing Turkish filigree.

This view of the entrance shows only one of the many versions of stained glass and paneling throughout the house. This and the view on the lower left are of the elaborate front staircase starting from an octagonal hall and centering on the tower windows over the porte cochere. The charming curved railing of the service stairs is on the lower right.

There is a wonderful romantic quality about these pictures. Though not an area had been spared embellishment, it was beautifully done. Even the dormers had a small carved animal at the window head.

DOCTOR HENRY E. JONES, who built this house on the site now occupied by St. Mary's Cathedral, came to Oregon in 1874 to be a military surgeon at Fort Stevens at the Columbia River's mouth. After six months in the service he resigned and started his medical practice in Portland. In later years he was chief surgeon at St. Vincent's Hospital and one of the most prominent physicians in the area. Mrs. Jones was the widow of Thomas A. Savier, a very successful flour and grain merchant and one of the very early pioneers of the city. The house faced Seventeenth Street with elaborate planting and gardens taking up most of the block. Down the street (in the right of this picture) is the south side of the Knapp house. Through the block are interesting versions of town houses: three residences joined by a common wall with gardens in front and rear; they also show in the pictures of the Williams house and are still standing, though they have been moved closer to the street.

There was a little architectural merit to the Jones house. All the unfortunate ugliness of Victorian taste seems to have been assembled in one massive jumble by the architect Joseph Sherwin. It was the gaiety and hospitality that took place here that remained in persons' minds long after those little pointed gable ends vanished.

The carriage entrance to the Henry Jones residence at the corner of Seventeenth and Davis streets.

The front parlor of the Jones residence.

THIS STRANGE STICK-STYLE RESIDENCE was directly behind the Henry Jones house. The doctor built it for his eldest step-daughter (Laura V. Savier) when she married Samuel M. Mears. It was on the northeast corner of Eighteenth and Couch, exactly where the main entrance to St. Mary's Cathedral is today. The board sidewalks and the absence of any planting around either house places the time about 1890. It is doubtful if planting would have helped such a forbidding looking place. Aside from the brackets the only breaks in simplicity were the stick divisions in the siding. The somber side of Victorian life seems to show in the stained glass window panes and the heavy barge board gable ends. Even the drawing of the house in the Panorama (p. 7) creates this strange feeling.

THIS DELIGHTFUL WEDDING CAKE (designed by Joseph Sherwin) was in direct contrast to the dour design of the Jones house. The turned gable ends were borrowed directly from romantic Bavarian sources and reproduced in wood. The unfortunate tower over the main entrance spoilt the continuity of the design, for the gable ends were even duplicated in the ornament at the top of the porte cochere.

This house was the home of the Honorable George H. Williams and was occupied about 1885. The entrance was on Eighteenth Street, and the driveway faced Couch. A glimpse of the buildings of the Bishop Scott Academy may be seen behind the house. In 1853 George H. Williams received a presidential appointment as the chief justice for the Oregon Territory, which brought him and his wife to this area. In 1864 he was elected to the United States Senate. President Grant appointed him attorney general, which made him a member of the cabinet. Later Grant nominated him for chief justice of the Supreme Court, an appointment that caused a storm of protest and rejection by the Senate. In 1902 Williams was elected mayor of Portland.

Despite the startling effect this picture gives at first impression, the house had a fine sense of proportion and scale. There was a grandeur about it that could only be understood if one could have seen a landau and pair arrive in that amazing porte cochere.

RT. REV. B. WISTAR MORRIS

The house on the northeast corner of Twentieth and Everett streets that belonged to the Rt. Rev. B. Wistar Morris, who for thirty-eight years was the episcopal bishop for Oregon. An apartment house now occupies the property.

Where the Biltmore Apartments now stand was the site of this large shingle house. It was the home of E. J. DeHart whose business later became the Honeyman Hardware Co. The entrance faced Twentieth Street and the side was on Glisan.

THE BLOCK of Nineteenth to Twentieth streets, Everett to Flanders, was the property of Mary Couch, Captain Couch's youngest daughter. Mary H. Couch never married and lived most of her mature years in Paris, where she was constant hostess to a stream of Portland travelers. Younger members of the family developed the Nineteenth Street half of the block with four handsome houses, each on a 100 by 100 foot plot. In the 1960s the four houses came down to make way for a federally-financed housing development. The two houses that faced Nineteenth Street belonged to Dr. Holt C. Wilson and C. Hunt Lewis and were designed by the architectural firm of Whidden and Lewis. The Wilson house was built in 1891 and the Lewis house in the same decade. They were interesting examples of the Colonial revival taking place at the time and of Whidden and Lewis' early work, which was definitely in that style. They had rather similar plans, with a large stair hall in the center of the house and two rooms opening on either side.

The other two houses were designed by David Chambers Lewis, a Couch grandson (no relation to Ion Lewis of Whidden and Lewis) who had an architectural practice in Portland. The pictures on the next page are of a house that was built in 1902 for his brother Robert W. Lewis. It was a comfortable, sensible house with the typical center hall plan. At the turn of the century the taste of the time moved toward a revival of Colonial simplicity from the romantic turrets and gables of Victorianism. The Robert Lewis house exemplified that change well.

The Robert W. Lewis residence on Everett Street.

THE HOLT C. WILSON HOUSE, mentioned earlier (p. 29), was located on the northwest corner of Nineteenth and Everett streets. The elaborate detail of quoin corner boards and heavy cornices, which were Whidden and Lewis trademarks, can be seen at the right edge of the early photograph (opposite, top). The snapshot above, taken just before the place was demolished, shows the sad state into which some of these houses fell. The "rope" cornice under the eaves was gone and the handsome trim around the windows was drowned in new shingles. Where the car was parked a one-story pavilion with the same fine detail had been removed; it housed a billiard room and opened onto a wide terrace that surrounded three sides of the house. This terrace, with its classic railings, gave the house a pedestal to sit on just as the black shutters, which had been removed, would have relieved the starkness of the snapshot. Age was not kind to this house, for all its fine qualities were stripped off with only a box remaining.

Unfortunately there is no picture available of the C. Hunt Lewis house, which faced Nineteenth Street alongside the Wilson house. It too was a Colonial revival design.

THE PICTURE OPPOSITE is a very early view of the fourth house of the group. It was built in 1905 for Stewart B. Linthicum, a law partner of George H. Williams and C. E. S. Wood. It was the first time David C. Lewis designed a residence in the English style of half timbering, and it became the prototype for houses all over Portland. The side was turned to Flanders Street and the entrance faced a lawn. In later years the hedge grew quite high and the planting matured, producing a beautiful, secluded garden.

THE VIEW OF THE ENTRANCE shows an interesting use of materials, shingles below and stucco above in the half timbering. For many years this was the home of Mr. and Mrs. Lee Hawley Hoffman.

IN 1905 WHIDDEN AND LEWIS designed this large mansion for Isam White, on the same site as the Couch house (opposite). Isam and Levi White (the latter's house is shown on p. 79) were prosperous merchants who came to Portland from Germany in 1858. The house was an interesting step in the design progress of Whidden and Lewis' architectural work. William M. Whidden came to Portland from the New York offices of McKim, Mead & White around 1899. He formed a practice with Ion Lewis, another New Yorker, that lasted into the First World War.

THE PICTURE ON THE OPPOSITE PAGE is of the house that the Couch family built on the northwest corner of Twentieth and Everett streets. This is a very old picture that shows wooden sidewalks and the dairy farm (in the right background) that straddled Cornell Road. The house had a bracketed flavor to it with simple stick-style ornament on the porch and eaves. It was occupied by members of the Wilson and Burns families until it was moved to Irving Street.

WHIDDEN AND LEWIS' early residential work showed the direct influence of Charles F. McKim, of the New York firm McKim, Mead & White, but later developed into a formal, classic type of design, of which the Isam White house is typical. All their favorite devices are here with the same balustraded terrace on three sides that was lost from the Wilson house, the raised cornice at the dormers to give a full third floor, and the absolute balance of proportions on the facade.

The plan differs from their other center hall houses because an enormous reception hall stretches across two-thirds of the front. It is paneled in hardwood with heavy hardwood pilasters on all four sides. From this a great balustraded staircase sweeps up to the second floor past a row of beautifully leaded windows.

These two recent views of the house show the excellent care that it has been given.

THE GEORGE F. HEUSNER RESIDENCE at 95 North Twentieth Street. This house, designed by Edgar M. Lazarus, and built at the turn of the century, is an excellent example of the shingle style of domestic architecture that came into vogue at the time. There is a very romantic feeling in the sweeping roofs, the old world tower, and the rough stone chimneys; it was hard to leave the Victorian elements. The porch changes course in its trip around the side and the square windowpanes change to diamond ones in the tower. This house is still standing and shares the block with the Isam White residence, making a striking pair of domiciles.

THIS WAS ONE OF THE GOOD EXAMPLES of a Victorian house that once graced northwest Portland. It was built on Everett Street for Captain John A. Brown. The heavy dormers, the tower shooting out of the circular porch, the disdain of proportion, were all architectural earmarks of the eighties. There was a playfulness and daring in the Thomas J. Jones design of this house that rather typified the brash ways of showing success at that time. The building has been razed, after much preservation effort in its favor.

CAPTAIN JOHN A. BROWN owned this dwelling west of his larger house. Though typical of its time the ornament and trim were much better than those used on the average Victorian cottage. The stone temple guard with an emperor's lotus emblem was a nice oriental touch. The building was razed in 1970.

ON THE CORNER of Twentieth Place and Everett Street is this large residence. Although one has the impression that too much is going on, the detailing, taken in separate parts, is excellent. The delicate frieze of circles at each window head, the leaf motif placed in the second floor paneling, and the egg-and-dart run in the rake mold are beautifully done. To top it all is the great carving in the gable end. No one seems to remember if the unfortunate band of plaster is a replacement for wood ornament. However, many do remember a handsome weathervane that topped the tower. This was the home of Gay Lombard who was the president of the Pacific Grain Co. Later the house belonged to General Thomas D. Anderson who occupied it with his son-in-law's family, the Charles Gaulds.

THE PERIOD OF ROMANTICISM came to the neighborhood in the Whidden and Lewis designed Mackenzie residence on the corner of Twentieth and Hoyt streets. Built of stone with a slate roof it is as handsome a house now as when it was new. The windows over the entrance arches and the dormers facing Hoyt Street are reminiscent of architect Norman Shaw's London houses.

Dr. K.A.J. Mackenzie came to Portland from Canada. Brilliantly educated in Europe, he became a leading physician in the Portland area and a founder of the University of Oregon Medical School. When he built this house the strong, heavy designs of H.H. Richardson were popular on the eastern seaboard and the architects Whidden and Lewis used many of those features on this exterior. There is a wealth of fine carving (by Nicholas Strahan) and paneling in the interior and a magnificent staircase. These beautiful rooms have been kept very much as they were by the Episcopal Laymen's Mission Society, which operates the property as the William Temple House, a counseling and assistance center.

THE VIEWS on the following pages are of the houses on Nineteenth Street from Flanders to Johnson. All the views are looking south from Johnson Street and were taken by Rodney Glisan from the third floor porch of the Josiah Myrick residence. The first picture, obviously the oldest from the size of the planting as well as the board sidewalks, encompasses the dwellings of most of Captain Couch's family. The first house on the left was owned by his brother-in-law George H. Flanders. The next, the large house with the tower, belonged to a daughter (Clementine), Mrs. Cicero H. Lewis, Sr. In front of it was the Walter J. Burns residence (Mrs. Burns was Couch's granddaughter, Mary Caroline Wilson), and on the right the residence of another daughter (Elizabeth), Mrs. Rodney Glisan. To the left of the Glisan house and behind it is a very small portion of the Robert Bruce Wilson house; still another daughter (Caroline). All of these houses were built between 1881 and 1885. Captain Couch gave his brother-in-law and each of his daughters a 200 by 400 foot block of his land claim from Everett Street to Johnson Street. His unmarried daughter (Mary), whose block was from Everett to Flanders streets, was the only one who did not build a large house at this time. Mrs. Burns was the daughter of the Wilsons, and that block was divided between the two families.

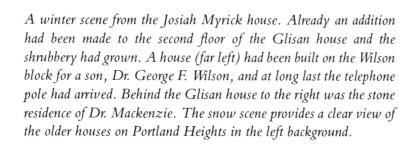

A winter scene from the Josiah Myrick house. Already an addition had been made to the second floor of the Glisan house and the shrubbery had grown. A house (far left) had been built on the Wilson block for a son, Dr. George F. Wilson, and at long last the telephone pole had arrived. Behind the Glisan house to the right was the stone residence of Dr. Mackenzie. The snow scene provides a clear view of the older houses on Portland Heights in the left background.

48

A still later picture of Nineteenth Street. The sidewalks had been paved but the streets were still unsurfaced. The luxuriant growth that the area became famous for was well underway.

The photographer turned slightly to the west for this picture, which obviously is a mate to the one on the preceding page. Starting from the Glisan house in the left background there is the dim outline of the Levi White house (where the present Couch School now stands) next to the stone tower of the Mackenzie residence —both facing on Twentieth Street. The large Victorian pile in the center was a house the Louis Lang family lived in, which burned down in the early nineteen hundreds. The portion of a building in the right foreground was the Mathias Koshland house on the northeast corner of Nineteenth and Johnson streets (which was later moved to its present location on Kearney Street).

THIS WAS THE RODNEY GLISAN HOUSE, so prominent in previous pictures. The view opposite must have been during the first year the family occupied it; the trees that later engulfed it have just been set out and the windows are curtainless. This is the only view of the Robert Bruce Wilson house (in the background) that shows how enormous it was. The pictures in the later pages show only portions of the Glisan house as the planting literally became a forest.

The Glisan residence was a rather grim house. The proportions were poor and the detailing seemed to have been tacked on. The gardens that took up the double block were as fine as the city had and in later years almost hid the house from the street.

Dr. Rodney Glisan came to Oregon as an army surgeon in 1855, having just graduated from the University of Maryland. He was first sent to Fort Orford and from there to Fort Yamhill (then commanded by Phil Sheridan, who later gained fame in the Civil War). Glisan resigned in 1861 and began a practice in Portland. For many years he was professor of obstetrics at the medical school and was always a leader in the state medical society. In 1863 he married Elizabeth Couch. In the city directories the first listing of this address was in 1855, very soon after the area was subdivided. Dr. Glisan's children, Caroline, Florence (Mrs. Arthur Minott), Dr. Clarence, and Rodney (a prominent attorney), occupied the house until it was torn down in the early thirties.

View of carriage entrance to the Glisan house, winding in from Twentieth Street to the rear of the house.

The Rodney Glisan residence from the corner
of Nineteenth and Irving.

PEOPLE WHO ADMIRE the Temple Beth Israel on Nineteenth and Flanders streets usually mention the beautiful, carefully preserved planting that gives the building its setting. It originated around this house, which occupied the same site. It was built for Captain George H. Flanders who was Captain Couch's brother-in-law. At the age of twenty-eight, Flanders came to Portland from Newburyport, Massachusetts, with Captain Couch. Flanders remained in the city and operated a series of docks and is credited with building one of the first brick buildings on Front Street.

Discounting its size, this Justus Krumbein design was sturdier and stronger than many of the Victorian houses around it. Some of the details were excellent, such as the interesting porch railing. The Flanders daughters (M. Louise and Caroline W.) lived in the house until Beth Israel purchased the property around 1930. A son, John Couch Flanders, built and occupied for many years a house on the rear of the property, where the Temple Beth Israel is presently located.

The Cicero H. Lewis residence.

CICERO H. LEWIS, SR., came from New Jersey to Portland in 1850. Like Henry W. Corbett, William S. Ladd, and Henry Failing, all of whom arrived at the same time, he became one of the merchant princes of the Northwest. In 1857 he married Captain Couch's second daughter, Clementine, and for many years they lived in a pleasant house on Fourth and Everett streets. In 1881 they built this house on the block bounded by Nineteenth, Twentieth, Glisan, and Hoyt streets. It was a very large house with stables, a greenhouse in the rear, and a long, sweeping drive to a porte cochere on the north.

The exterior was an interesting version of the bracketed stick-style at its best. The wide overhang of the rake and eaves was supported by brackets and a lacy grillwork that was quite unusual. The gable end over the handsome two-story bay was a beautifully proportioned architectural composition.

THOUGH THE EXTERIOR OF THE LEWIS HOUSE was rather simple for its period, the interior was much more elaborate. Rare woods, marble mantels, brocaded walls, fine lighting fixtures, were used throughout the house. To the left of the front entrance were the usual front and rear parlors, the rear one used as a library. To the right was a reception room with a beautiful marble fireplace. Behind this was the massive stairway and the carriage entrance. The carved trim of the door heads and the tall windows provided a touch of elegance that set off a mixture of objects and fine furnishings.

Eleven children were born to the Lewises, all of whom at some time lived in this house. After the family was gone the house was razed and the property developed into a playground for Couch School.

The entrance hall and staircase of the Lewis residence.

In the northwest corner of the Lewis residence was a reception room, shown here. The wainscot was a material treated to look like metal and used again at the cornice over the handsome paper frieze. The window shutters, which folded back into their own pockets, were

typical of Victorian houses; the swags over the windows were kept short to not interfere with them. Probably the finest workmanship in the house was the beautiful inlaid floor. The view above shows the drawing room.

A drawing room and parlor with a dining room behind them occupied the south side of the Lewis house. The view opposite is toward the front bay windows and the other views the entrance and fireplace wall

of the parlor. All the rooms had very elaborate overmantels of mirror and millwork. The dentil course over the doors was particularly noteworthy.

The bedroom over the drawing room
in the Lewis residence.

SOON AFTER THIS HOUSE of Robert Bruce Wilson's was built it was engulfed in a forest of fir trees. Very few pictures show its size or detailing. The house was backed against Twentieth Street on the corner of Hoyt, and a winding drive came in from Nineteenth Street. In later years a son, George F., built a house on the Nineteenth Street end of the property. Robert Bruce Wilson was one of the first doctors in Portland, coming from Virginia in 1850. He was a physician of education and training and made a prominent place for himself in the community. With the active part he took in the civic life of the growing city, he was felt by many to be the dean of the medical profession.

Mrs. Wilson was Captain Couch's eldest daughter. Two of the Wilson sons, Holt C. and George F., became leading physicians in Portland in their generation. This house was built about the time of the other Couch houses around it, the family having lived for years on the corner of Fourth and Burnside. The Wilson house has been gone since the late twenties; apartment houses now cover the entire block.

The front entrance of the R. B. Wilson house, at the end of the long driveway; vines at right covered a large, three-storied wing.

*The rear of the Wilson house from the corner of
Twentieth and Hoyt streets.*

WALTER J. BURNS, who built this house, was the head of Balfour, Guthrie, the British grain firm. Mrs. Burns was the daughter of R.B. Wilson, whose house is directly behind in this picture. The Lewis house is to the left and the DeHart house is in the left distance. It is a very early photograph; the sidewalks were wooden and the streets unimproved. In the distance a pasture on the steep rise that was for many years the location of St. Vincent's Hospital. This was a comfortable, livable-looking house, interestingly void of a great deal of the embellishment of its neighbors. The jigsaw work on the gable ends was beautifully done.

12256

THE FLANDERSES BUILT THIS HOUSE on the rear of their property for their son John Couch Flanders. In later years it was the home of J. N. Teal's mother and sister, until it was pulled down for an apartment house. Interim occupants were the Linthicum family.

THIS UNFORTUNATELY DESIGNED HOUSE was built on the front part of the R. B. Wilson property and faced Nineteenth Street at Hoyt. It represents the struggle of architectural styles that achieve only a conglomeration. The fenestration was very poor and the heavy dormers and gable ends were completely out of scale. This was the home of Dr. George Flanders Wilson, Dr. Robert Bruce Wilson's son.

THIS CHARMING LITTLE BUILDING is still standing on Hoyt Street between Twentieth and Twenty-First. It was built in the 1890s by the Couch family as a schoolhouse for all their grandchildren and other children in the neighborhood. One of the first teachers was Susan Piper, who later became Mrs. Henry Hewett. It was made into a residence about 1920 and for years was the home of Madam Reed of the Catlin School French department.

The residence of Dr. Ernest F. Tucker on Hoyt Street between Twentieth and Twenty-First.

THIS HOUSE was built in 1881 by Frederick Alleyne Beck, whose wife (Sarah H. Piper) was a niece of Captain Couch. Like the Captain, Beck had brought his family from Newburyport, Massachusetts to settle in Portland. It was a simple, straightforward house rather typical of houses built all over the city at the time. There was no central heating system, only fireplaces, but the Becks had the first enamel-iron bathtub ever installed in a Portland residence.

In 1900 Dr. Ernest F. Tucker purchased the house from his father-in-law. Whidden and Lewis made extensive additions and alterations to house the Tucker family, one a handsome library with a great inglenook fireplace.

Dr. Tucker was a staff member of St. Vincent's Hospital where he lectured on gynecology. For many years he held the chair of anatomy at the medical school. Out of this house came the present generation of Tuckers, Biddles, Malarkeys, and Livingstones.

THE PICTURES on this and the opposite page are of the Henry Hewett house on the site of the present Couch School. When the Hewett family left this house they developed an upland farm on Hewett Boulevard in the area that is now Green Hills. This house was moved around the corner to a site in the middle of the block on Hoyt Street, leaving the property for the Levi Whites. Henry Hewett's first and second wives (Frances and Susan) were both members of the Piper family, and were nieces of Captain Couch.

THE OPPOSITE PICTURE is a very old one taken before either Glisan or Hoyt streets were cut through. The photographer had a fine time posing all the Couch grandchildren on the circular driveway. The house had a typical T-shaped plan and the exterior was like dozens of other early houses in the city. To distinguish it from the others some ornament was added over the windows and a fine railing was built over the porch. The windmill in the rear gives evidence that this was one of the few houses that did not receive its water from the river. Old panoramas of Portland show this house to be about the first one in the area.

The Henry Hewett residence.

The Levi White residence.

THIS GREAT VICTORIAN PILE was razed before the First World War to make way for the present Couch School building. It was the Levi White residence that faced Twentieth Street between Glisan and Hoyt. It occupied the site of the Hewett house and might have been on the same foundation. It was a huge house with every form of jigsaw ornament on it. The elliptical tower, with part of another tower imposed on it, was an unusual feature even in this era of domestic architecture when everything was tried. After the Whites left the house it became Dr. Robert C. Coffey's North Pacific Sanitorium until it was pulled down.

A VERY EARLY VIEW of the G.V. James residence, which occupied the block between Eighteenth, Nineteenth, Irving
and Johnson streets. The entrance shown here faced east
toward Eighteenth Street. The Cicero H. Lewis residence
appears in the left background and beyond are the West Hills.
James was the manager of the Oregon Transfer Co., and lived
in the house until about 1895, when it was occupied by
Brigadier General Charles F. Beebe and his family.

A LATER VIEW of the James house from Eighteenth Street taken in 1890. The house was built in 1880 and was an excellent example of the Italianate style so popular then. The ornate porch and the embellishment over the windows were the typical additions to a simple style of architecture. In the early 1900s the block was divided and the Koehler residence was built on the north half. The entrance of the latter faced Nineteenth Street and a beautiful garden was developed (to the right of this picture). An apartment house now occupies the site.

RICHARD KOEHLER was a native of Germany who came to Portland to represent the Villard railroad interests. For most of his years in the city he was connected with the railroad business. Around 1905 the firm of Whidden and Lewis designed this house for him at the southeast corner of Nineteenth and Johnson streets. The same open terrace on the front of the house stretches across the rear, and once faced a fine enclosed garden that is now gone. The beautiful simplicity of the formal facade was rather spoilt by the baluster rail at the roof. Fortunately time has removed it and the effect is one of improvement (opposite illustration). The house is now used for commercial and professional offices.

THESE TWO VERY EARLY PICTURES of the Myrick residence, probably were taken at the same time. The house was built on the northeast corner of Nineteenth and Johnson streets about 1887. Josiah Myrick was a mine owner and a steamboat captain who came around the Horn in 1852. His wife was M. Louisa Rae, Dr. John McLoughlin's granddaughter. It was a solid, pleasant residence, typical of the Victorian houses across the country but void of a great deal of the jigsaw ornament of the period. The two Myrick daughters, Elizabeth and Winifrid, lived in the house until their deaths in the late 1940s, when it was torn down.

THE VIEW OPPOSITE is the east side of the house with a third floor porch, which must have given a sweeping view of the city and harbor before the shade trees were planted. The "aerial" views down Nineteenth Street (pp. 44-51) were taken from this porch by Rodney Glisan. The house in the left background of the picture is the Perkins-Koshland house built in 1887 and moved away when the W. B. Ayer house was built on the same site. Between the two houses can be seen a small building with a strange cupola; it was a stable shared by the Bacon and Weidler residences, which faced on Nineteenth Street. In the right distance is the Prescott house on Lovejoy Street.

THE SNOW SCENE, a much later picture of the Myrick house, shows, on the right, the Shea house, which faced on Johnson Street and is still standing, and the N. Edward Ayer house on the left. The Ayer house was designed by Whidden and Lewis in 1900 and was an excellent example of the shingle style. It faced Nineteenth Street and an elaborate garden ran back to Eighteenth. Before it was torn down for a service station it was occupied for many years by the Benjamin Keator family.

THE HANDSOME SHEA RESIDENCE was built about 1890 on the rest of the quarter block next to the Myrick house. It faces Johnson Street at the corner of Eighteenth and is still standing. This was the first residence that W. B. Ayer occupied before he built the larger house at Nineteenth and Johnson; both houses were designed by Whidden and Lewis. The sudden turn to the classic style of domestic design was startling. Only a few years before the height had been reached in stick-style, bracketed Gothic and Victorian jigsaw. This house has grace and dignity from its pleasant bow windows to the well-proportioned dormers. For many years it was the home of the John F. Shea family, and in between the Ayers and the Sheas it was occupied by T. W. B. London, the head of Balfour, Guthrie. It is still in excellent condition and behind its high hedge is a pleasant oasis in a commercial neighborhood.

THE NORTHWEST CORNER of Nineteenth and Johnson streets was occupied by this house before the W. B. Ayer house was built. It was the residence of Richard S. Perkins, an eastern Oregon cattleman who built the Perkins Hotel. Prior to 1905, after it had become the Mathias Koshland house, it was moved around the corner to Kearney Street where it is still standing. On this latter site it has been a private home, an apartment house, and is now occupied by professional offices. A surprising number of houses of this and earlier periods were moved rather than torn down. A minimum of overhead wires and an absence of elaborate plumbing systems made it a fairly easy task.

The Winslow B. Ayer house.

WINSLOW B. AYER built this handsome house at Nineteenth and Johnson streets in 1905. It ranked among the finest houses of the city at the time and was an architectural gem that Whidden and Lewis could take great pride in. The rather severe Georgian style is made domestic by the lovely window detail, the mellow brick work, and the excellent overall proportions. There is a scholarly dignity and a sense of returning to normal taste after decades of the bizarre.

The Ayers were New Englanders of wealth and taste who filled the house with treasures of paintings and furnishings. Their unerring sense of the right thing showed best in the possession of French Impressionist paintings at a time when they were not too well received. Mr. Ayer's contributions and great interest in the collection of the Portland Art Museum and the housing of the Public Library have been invaluable to both institutions down through the years.

These pictures, and the views of the Koehler house, which is across the intersection, show how at that time this section of Portland resembled some Boston suburbs.

NEXT DOOR TO THE AYER RESIDENCE, and occupying the rest of the block, was this pleasant house of Mr. and Mrs. George Good. It was also designed by Whidden and Lewis, but was built a good ten years earlier than the Ayer house. Mr. Good was an investment broker and the manager of the Bank of British Columbia. His wife was a daughter of Cicero H. Lewis, Sr., and a granddaughter of Captain Couch. Again there is a strong borrowing from the English domestic architects such as Guy Dawber and Norman Shaw. The rolled pediment of the side dormer and the broken gable end are marks of a "Queen Anne" style developed at this time. The exterior is done in odd-sized bricks that were fired in England and shipped to Portland for this house. This and its neighbor made a striking pair of residences, both excellent in architectural taste and in design.

The Good house as it was in 1910 (above) and in the 1960s (below).

THE W. HARRISON CORBETT RESIDENCE on Kearney Street behind the Good house. This is an interesting example of the shingle cottage style popular around 1910, here turned into a city house. A dormer over the entrance, that gave the design a better sense of proportion, has been removed. In later years the house was occupied by the D.W.L. MacGregor family.

THIS DRAWING shows one of the very early houses of the area, located on the northwest corner of Twentieth and Johnson streets and completed in 1881. It was the home of John C. Carson, a pioneer lumberman, and for many years president of the state senate. The house was torn down around 1910 and replaced by the Veness residence, shown on the following pages.

HON. J. C. CARSON

EMIL SCHACHT was a successful Portland architect who designed many fine residences. His drawings of this house reproduced here are from the 1908 yearbook of the Portland Architectural Club. The house was built around 1910 on the site of the J. C. Carson house, and the design was borrowed directly from the Dutch colonial farms of Long Island and the Hudson River Valley. Unfortunately it is a type of house that should have been in a country setting rather than a crowded city corner.

From 1911 to 1916 it was occupied by the Charles H. Davis family and after that for many years it was the home of John A. Veness, a lumberman. Today it belongs to a church society.

"BEFORE AND AFTER" could be the title for these two pages. In 1905 this simple Dutch colonial city house was built for Mrs. Edward Failing. It is located directly in back of the Ayer garden on Johnson Street. The house was very new in the above picture and served as a backdrop to the elaborate grounds of the Rodney Glisan residence. Mrs. Failing's daughter, Henrietta, lived here for many years.

THE VIEW on the opposite page shows all that is left behind the brick wall that surrounded the garden.

THIS HANDSOME GEORGIAN TOWN HOUSE was the Abbot L. Mills residence on the southwest corner of Twentieth and Johnson streets. It was built in 1908 by the Boston architectural firm of Shepley, Rutan and Coolidge. The same firm later designed the First National Bank for Mr. Mills, who was president at that time.

Another house, for many years the Mills house, occupied the rear part of this property, and was designed by Whidden and Lewis; it was one of their first commissions after completing the Portland Hotel. When the house pictured here was finished and family installed, the old house behind it was torn down.

Though New England in character, the inspiration for this design came from several old Philadelphia houses that the Millses were familiar with, one, especially in Germantown. It is definitely a town house, set very near the sidewalk with a fine formal garden at the rear. The house has lost the domestic quality of a fine residence; it needs the great elms that were in the parking strip, the English ivy on the brickwork, and the louvered shutters that broke the harshness of the gable ends. But it is fortunate that it still stands.

When the family left the house it was purchased by the Catholic Archdiocese of Portland and for many years was the residence of the archbishop. After the archdiocese established a new residence the property was converted into professional offices.

The Abbot L. Mills house.

THE ABBOT MILLSES had three sons. One of them, the late Lewis H. Mills, built this house on Irving Street. Like the senior Mills residence it was designed by Shepley, Rutan and Coolidge, with the feeling of a town residence hemmed in on the sides by other houses. The two Mills houses shared the large garden between them. The design is simple New England colonial with a center hall plan and a completely wood exterior, one concession the Boston architects made to the Far West.

The house was erected in 1916, and in 1936 Mr. and Mrs. Mills stripped it for a country residence they built in Dunthorpe. All the fine exterior trim, from the fan light doorway shown on this page, to the widow's walk, were incorporated in the new house. Likewise, paneled walls, fireplace mantels, stair rails and doors were taken from the interior. Needless to say the newer house in the open fields of Military Road is a masterpiece of fine detail work.

The remaining shell on Irving Street is today used for offices.

Doorway to the Lewis H. Mills residence.

The Lewis H. Mills residence.

The Lewis H. Mills house in 1968.

NOT ALL OF WHIDDEN AND LEWIS' WORK consisted of elaborate mansions and public buildings. This simple, straightforward house was built for John Kiernan in 1905 and exemplified comfort and good taste. The house shared Twentieth Street with the Abbot L. Mills residence, which shows to the right. The Russell Hubbard family occupied the house through most of its years. Today the site is an elaborate apartment complex aptly called "Hubbard House."

PROBABLY NO HOUSE PICTURED in this volume was more amazing than the one here. No matter how long one studies the facade it seems that something new and strange is found. Only the Charles Forbes house that stood on Vista Avenue and Park Place could claim the distinction of dripping with more ornament. This house was on Irving Street between the Lewis H. Mills and the Hubbard houses, and was built by William S. Mason, mayor of Portland in 1892-93. He was also president of the Portland National Bank and a partner in Mason, Ehrman & Co. The second owner was John Kiernan who lived in it until he built the house next door (shown on the opposite page). It was then occupied by a Kiernan son-in-law, Russell B. Caswell, and his family.

The strange base that supported the bay, the keyhole window that must have been a glazier's delight, the lonely, second floor medallion, were only a few of the things that were happening in this fanciful composition. The imagination that went into this exterior created something daring and wonderful.

THE NEW YORK ARCHITECTURAL FIRM of McKim, Mead & White did several large summer residences at Newport, Rhode Island. Whidden and Lewis, who came from that firm, brought this flavor to the domestic work they did in Portland, and their house on these pages was very much in character with the East Coast structures. There was a definite sophistication in the facade and in both the floor plans shown on the following pages. There was also a harking back to London houses of the period in the twin chimney stacks and the vestibuled entrance set on the street. A delightful play of proportions took place in the composition of the first floor balancing the windows of the second floor.

There has been a criticism in this book that many of the large houses in this area deserved more room for a setting, but this was a perfect city house completely suited to its urban corner.

It was built in 1892, across the intersection from the Abbot L. Mills house at Twentieth and Johnson streets. Mr. Zera Snow, the owner, was a prominent attorney and law partner of Judge Wallace McCamant. The Snow family lived here until 1908 when the house was purchased by the lumberman Edwin Shevlin. It was during the Shevlins' occupancy that the beautiful gardens in the rear were developed to maturity; surrounded by a brick wall they extended for almost a city block. After Mr. Shevlin's death it became a boarding house and then was torn down in the late 1950s.

The plans reproduced on the following pages are from the original Whidden and Lewis blueprints used during the construction of the house.

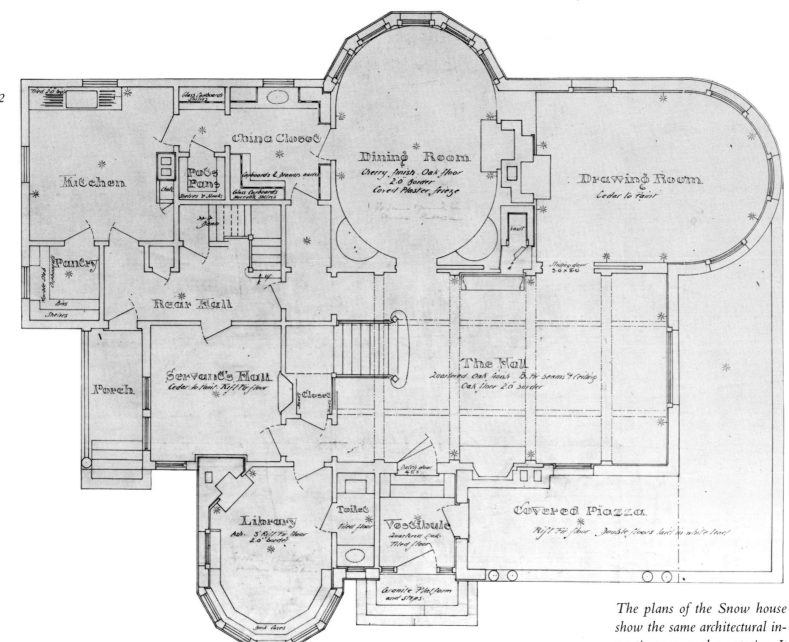

Kitchen

China Closet

Pots & Pans

Dining Room
Cherry finish. Oak floor
2.0" Border
Cored Plaster Frieze

Drawing Room
Cedar to paint

Pantry

Rear Hall

Porch

Servant's Hall
Cedar to paint. Rift Fir floor

The Hall
Quartered Oak finish B. Fir beams & ceiling
Oak floor 2.0" border

Closet

Library
Ash. 3 Rift Fir floor
2.0" border

Toilet
tiled floor

Vestibule
Quartered Oak
Tiled floor

Covered Piazza
Rift Fir floor. Double floors laid in white lead

Granite Platform
and steps.

The plans of the Snow house
show the same architectural in-
ventiveness as the exterior. It
was a luxurious house made for
the formal living and entertain-
ing of the nineties. There was
an English idea of a great hall
paneled in quartered oak, with a

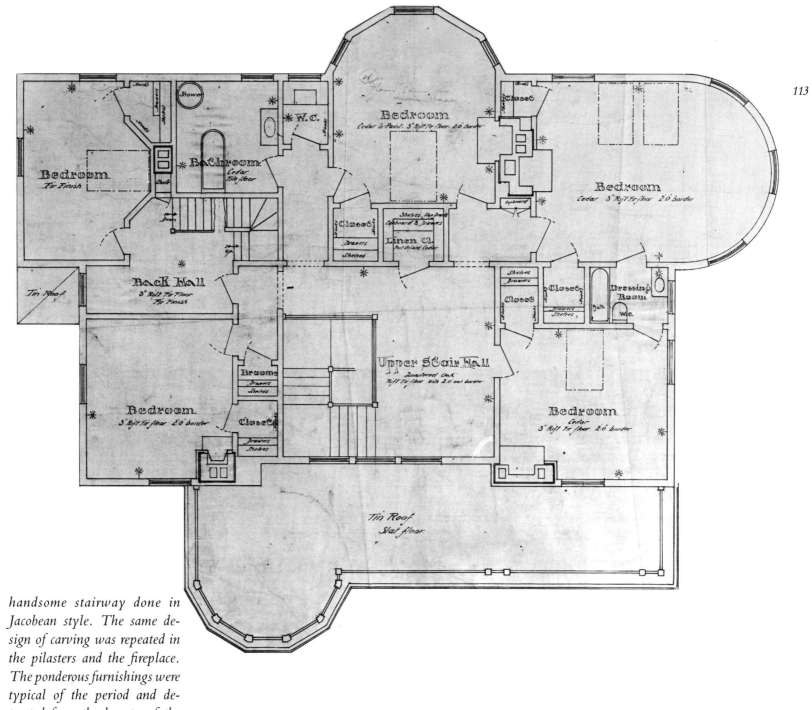

Bedroom
Fir Finish

Bathroom
Cedar
Tile floor

Shower

W.C.

Bedroom
Cedar to Paint. 3" Rift Fir floor. 2'0 border

Closet

Bedroom
Cedar 3" Rift Fir floor 2'0 border

Tin Roof

Back Hall
3" Rift Fir Floor
Fir Finish

Closet
Drawers
Shelves

Linen Cl.
Port Orford Cedar

Shelves, Hardwood
Cupboard & Drawers

Closet

Shelves
Drawers

Closet

Dressing
Room

Bath

W.C.

Bedroom
3" Rift Fir floor 2'0 border

Brooms
Drawers
Shelves

Closet

Upper Stair Hall
Quartered Oak
Rift Fir floor with 2'0 oak border

Bedroom
Cedar
3" Rift Fir floor 2'6 border

Drawers
Shelves

Tin Roof
Slat floor

handsome stairway done in Jacobean style. The same design of carving was repeated in the pilasters and the fireplace. The ponderous furnishings were typical of the period and detracted from the beauty of the room itself.

On one side of the main entrance and directly on the street was the library (opposite, top left). The walls were paneled in ash that was cut to show a pattern of graining. A brocade wallpaper went from this wainscot up to the ceiling. It was a pleasant, small family room void of the garish decorations of that time.

The children in front of the drawing room fireplace (right) are Berkeley and MacCormac Snow. There is a hazy view of the plaster cornice and ceiling decoration, which is almost a lost art.

The dining room in the Snow house (opposite, top right) was rather like the interior of a shell, for the shape was not only oval but the ceiling was coved to a plaster frieze in the center. Paneled in cherry with a reddish Italian marble fireplace it was a most effective room. The gas lighting fixtures throughout the house were fine pieces of craftsmanship.

This bedroom of the Snow house (opposite, bottom left) was over the dining room. The brass bed, the rattan chairs, the china washbowl were all typical furnishings of a fine nineteenth century house. The fireplace mantel had an excellent ornamental design worked on its face.

The design of the hall (opposite, lower right) was based on the great halls found in English country houses, off of which all important rooms opened. This room was beautifully paneled in quartered oak, and had a tall, marble fireplace. Later, when the Shevlins lived here, it was sparsely furnished as a hall should be, which gave emphasis to the hand—carved Jacobean-style staircase.

THE TWO HOUSES in the above illustration were on the double block of Nineteenth, Twentieth, Kearney and Lovejoy streets. They faced onto Nineteenth Street with drives through the 460 foot block to the stables on Twentieth Street. The version of a Florentine villa in the foreground was the Charles P. Bacon residence and the towered mansion beyond belonged to his son-in-law, George W. Weidler.

Charles Bacon came to Portland in 1855 as the Wells, Fargo agent and was one of the first city councilmen. The rear of this house shows in the picture of the Snow residence (p. 110). It was typical of the Italianate style except that the very wide trim around all the sash and the pointed Gothic window heads on the first floor were unusual.

THE GEORGE WEIDLER HOUSE is shown on the opposite page. It had an ungainly design with a full daylight basement that threw the whole house high in the air. Weidler was associated with Ben Holladay in extensive sawmill operations and in the first electric plant built in Portland. Both houses were designed by Warren H. Williams, and have been gone for many years.

THE DRAWINGS OF THE INTERIOR of the Prescott house done for the *West Shore* magazine show surroundings more typical of the nineties than the previous interiors illustrated in this book. From the time of the Civil War on, furniture styling and standards of decorating seem to have descended to an all-time low. Armed with the fear of not filling every niche and corner, and not caring if taste were used in the process, the "General Grant House" was reproduced all over America. There was no reason for these drawings to be in color for pleasant colors were almost sinful. A glance at the chairs and tables tells why so few Victorian furnishings were ever saved for coming generations. There are three fireplaces in these drawings; though conversation must have been as good then as today, there was no seating provided in front of any of the fireplaces. It is an interesting commentary that the imagination and workmanship that went into the exterior of Victorian houses seldom penetrated the front door. The Knapp house (illustrated at the beginning of this book) shows how fine interiors could be, but seldom were.

Charles H. Prescott was the president of the Oregon Railroad and Navigation Co., and later was vice president of the Northern Pacific. He built this house for his family in 1884 on a large plot of ground on Lovejoy Street above Nineteenth. It was torn down in the 1960s for an expansion of the Physician and Surgeons Hospital. The Prescotts lived here for only four years and then it became the home of the Samuel Heitshu family. Their daughter Alice later married John C. Ainsworth, the president of the United States National Bank. Next to this place was the Frank Knapp residence, shown on the following pages. The two families were great friends and no definition was made between the properties. A great sweep of lawn surrounded the houses for almost two city blocks.

NEXT TO THE HEITSHU HOUSE and also facing Lovejoy Street was this house of Frank A. Knapp. Mrs. Knapp's first husband was John W. Brazee, an engineer who built the portage railroad at Cascade Locks in 1862. When he died in 1887, he left a large fortune including the St. Charles Hotel on Front and Madison streets — then the city's finest. This house was built in 1892 when Mrs. Brazee and Mr. Knapp were married.

The place was a departure from the Victorian houses of the same date; the beginning of a simple shingle style that was popular in the West for the next thirty years. It is interesting how the rear of this house had a gambrel roof that had nothing to do with the front design.

The house had a straightforward plan with a large central hall. From this hall rooms opened out in all four directions. There were a parlor and library on either side of the front entrance and a billiard room and a dining room at the two corners in the rear.

This house in later years became the Physicians and Surgeons Hospital. Two wings were added for expanding facilities and the circular drive became a court. Many persons will remember the entrance hall with its great open staircase, for it was the lobby of the hospital for years.

A pleasant summer day on the front porch of the Knapp house. The old Couch School at Eighteenth and Lovejoy streets is in the background.

This view of the entrance hall is from the front door. The parlor was on the left and the library to the right. The elaborate stairway split at the landing and went up either side to the second floor. A very fine leaded glass bay threw light down into the hall. Behind the stairs was a convenient carriage entrance. The amount of furniture crowded in is amazing and the lampshades are unbelievable.

The billiard room in the Knapp house.

The colonial revival in architectural styles is well illustrated in the fireplaces of this house. The one here in the parlor was less clumsy than the one in the front hall, but both show the return to the old Greek styles of ornamental detail. Again the furnishings were fussy and Victorian even to the "Turkish Corner" by the fireplace; this was a must in good interiors of the nineties.

THE PANORAMA in the front of this book has some of the first houses in the area, so it seems fitting to close with this one, which was one of the last to be built. The architect David C. Lewis made this his home. It is on Twenty-First and Pettygrove streets, and is now a business office. The graceful dormers, the wide rake board, the heavy cornice, make it an excellent reproduction of a Dutch Long Island farmhouse. It is too bad that no picture is available of the Mrs. Emma Lewis Bingham house on Eighteenth and Kearney that Mr. Lewis designed in the same style. Both houses had a timeless domestic quality that would have kept them as private homes in other parts of the city.

FINIS

We have come through a sentimental journey of old Portland, geographically, socially, and architecturally. Geographically we have started at Burnside Street, where Tanner Creek still flowed as an open stream, and moved toward long-gone Guild Lake. Socially we have moved with the growth of the city coupled with the ever American success story, for these were fine houses built with the returns from hard work in a new land. Architecturally it is the story of changing tastes, new styles, some copyism, and much invention.

Since this book was first published ten years ago a surge of interest has arisen in these houses. There has been an attempt to save what little is left of this area, and the styles and mode of living it represented. These houses were built by persons who left the crowded Eastern areas for the open West to start anew. There is no longer a frontier but we seem to have a new national desire to make a fresh start. Perhaps this is why we find the aroused interest in these old dwellings; they have an aura of firm family ties and a sense of security that we are searching for.

INDEX

(italicized numbers indicate illustrations)
(epm = endpaper map)

CREDITS

Oregon Historical Society, Pages 6-7
    (Panorama), 8, 12, 28, 35, 60, 79-81,
    88, 97-98, 116, 118-19
Misses Gladys and Helen Dunne, Page 9
Mrs. Dorothy Gill Montgomery, Page 10
Mr. Walter T. Williamson, Page 13
Mr. Alan de Lay, Pages 16-19
Mrs. Richard A. Shearer, Pages 22-24

Mrs. Erle F. Whitney, Page 30
Mr. Alexander W. Linthicum, Pages 32,
    53, 69, 72, 94
Mrs. Lee Hawley Hoffman, Pages 32, 34,
    71
Mr. William H. Grand, Pages 36-37,
    39-43, 73, 82, 86-87, 89-90, 93, 95-96,
    99, 101, 104, 107, 125

Portland Public Library, Pages 33, 38
Mr. Joseph A. Minott, Pages 44-52,
    55-57, 67-68, 83, 86, 91-92, 95, 100
Mr. F. Faber Lewis, Pages 58, 61-66
Mr. Ernest F. Tucker, Pages 74, 76-77
Mrs. David Lloyd Davies, Pages 84-85
Mr. John A. Mills, Page 102
Mrs. Hubbard Stevenson, Page 108

Mrs. Ronald J. Honeyman, Page 109
Mrs. MacCormac Snow, Pages 110-15
Mrs. Stanley G. Jewett, Page 117
Gift to the author from the late Mrs.
    Morton Insley, Pages 14, 21, 27, 78,
    120-23
Gift to the author from the late Mrs.
    Lewis Mills, Pages 105-106

The text and display typog-
raphy of this book are set in Mer-
genthaler Bembo, a modern version of
Francesco Griffo's design for the Aldus
Manutius publication of Pietro Cardinal Bembo's
De Aetna (1496). *Nineteenth Street* was composed by
Paul O. Giesey, Adcrafters, printed by Graphic Arts Center,
and bound by Lincoln and Allen of Portland. The text paper is
70# Colophon. The sewn-and-drawn paperbound edition is bound
in 10 pt. Husky C1S, and the hardcover is bound in Gane book cloth.
This edition was edited and re-designed by Bruce T. Hamilton.
(1968 edition designed by Charles S. Politz)
Special thanks to Thomas Vaughan and Arthur C. Spencer.

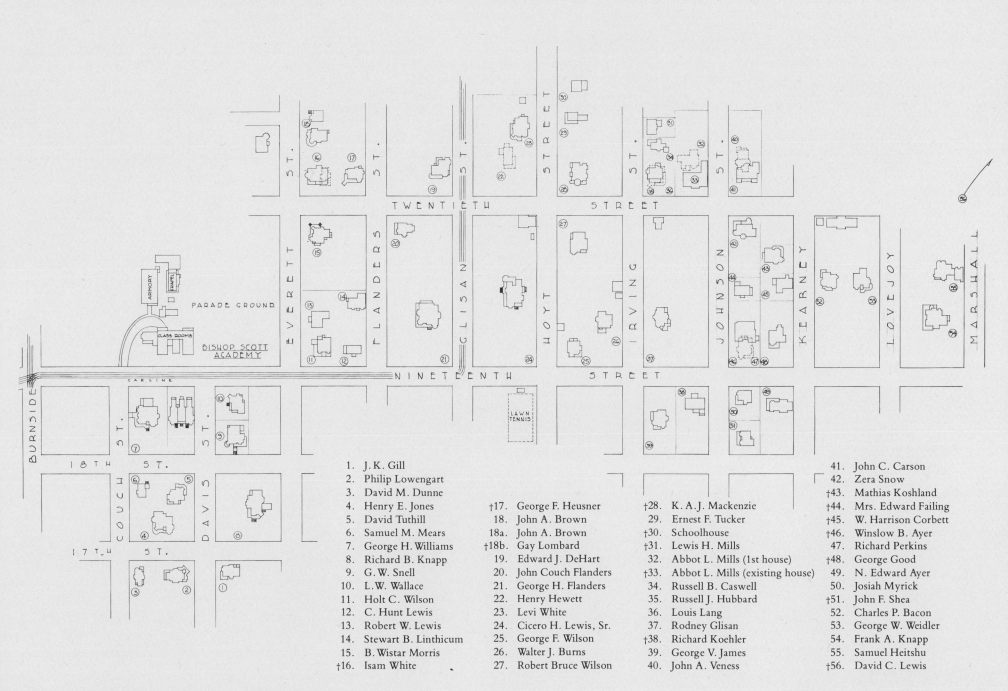

1. J. K. Gill
2. Philip Lowengart
3. David M. Dunne
4. Henry E. Jones
5. David Tuthill
6. Samuel M. Mears
7. George H. Williams
8. Richard B. Knapp
9. G. W. Snell
10. L. W. Wallace
11. Holt C. Wilson
12. C. Hunt Lewis
13. Robert W. Lewis
14. Stewart B. Linthicum
15. B. Wistar Morris
†16. Isam White

†17. George F. Heusner
18. John A. Brown
18a. John A. Brown
†18b. Gay Lombard
19. Edward J. DeHart
20. John Couch Flanders
21. George H. Flanders
22. Henry Hewett
23. Levi White
24. Cicero H. Lewis, Sr.
25. George F. Wilson
26. Walter J. Burns
27. Robert Bruce Wilson

†28. K. A. J. Mackenzie
29. Ernest F. Tucker
†30. Schoolhouse
†31. Lewis H. Mills
32. Abbot L. Mills (1st house)
†33. Abbot L. Mills (existing house)
34. Russell B. Caswell
35. Russell J. Hubbard
36. Louis Lang
37. Rodney Glisan
†38. Richard Koehler
39. George V. James
40. John A. Veness

41. John C. Carson
42. Zera Snow
†43. Mathias Koshland
†44. Mrs. Edward Failing
†45. W. Harrison Corbett
†46. Winslow B. Ayer
47. Richard Perkins
†48. George Good
49. N. Edward Ayer
50. Josiah Myrick
†51. John F. Shea
52. Charles P. Bacon
53. George W. Weidler
54. Frank A. Knapp
55. Samuel Heitshu
†56. David C. Lewis

†still standing